ISAAC ASIMOV'S NEW LIBRARY OF THE UNIVERSE

ASTRONOMY IN ANCIENT TIMES

BY ISAAC ASIMOV
WITH REVISIONS AND UPDATING BY FRANCIS REDDY

Gareth Stevens Publishing
MILWAUKEE

For a free color catalog describing Gareth Stevens' list of high-quality books, call 1-800-542-2595 (USA) or 1-800-461-9120 (Canada). Gareth Stevens' Fax: (414) 225-0377.

Library of Congress Cataloging-in-Publication Data

Asimov, Isaac.
   Astronomy in ancient times / by Isaac Asimov; with revisions
 and updating by Francis Reddy.
      p. cm. — (Isaac Asimov's New library of the universe)
   Rev. ed. of: Ancient astronomy. 1988.
   Includes bibliographical references and index.
   ISBN 0-8368-1191-7
   1. Astronomy, Ancient—Juvenile literature. [1. Astronomy, Ancient.]
 I. Reddy, Francis, 1959-. II. Asimov, Isaac. Ancient astronomy.
 III. Title. IV. Series: Asimov, Isaac. New library of the universe.
 QB16.A754 1995
 520'.93—dc20   94-31253

This edition first published in 1995 by
Gareth Stevens Publishing
1555 North RiverCenter Drive, Suite 201
Milwaukee, Wisconsin 53212, USA

Project editor: Barbara J. Behm
Design adaptation: Helene Feider
Editorial assistant: Diane Laska
Production director: Susan Ashley
Picture research: Kathy Keller
Artwork commissioning: Kathy Keller and Laurie Shock

Printed in the United States of America

5-95

1 2 3 4 5 6 7 8 9 99 98 97 96 95

To bring this classic of young people's information up to date, the editors at Gareth Stevens Publishing have selected two noted science authors, Greg Walz-Chojnacki and Francis Reddy. Walz-Chojnacki and Reddy coauthored the recent book *Celestial Delights: The Best Astronomical Events Through 2001.*

Walz-Chojnacki is also the author of the book *Comet: The Story Behind Halley's Comet* and various articles about the space program. He was an editor of *Odyssey,* an astronomy and space technology magazine for young people, for eleven years.

Reddy is the author of nine books, including *Halley's Comet, Children's Atlas of the Universe, Children's Atlas of Earth Through Time,* and *Children's Atlas of Native Americans,* plus numerous articles. He was an editor of *Astronomy* magazine for several years.

CONTENTS

We live in an enormously large place – the Universe. It's just in the last fifty-five years or so that we've found out how large it probably is. It's only natural that we would want to understand the place in which we live, so scientists have developed instruments – such as radio telescopes, satellites, probes, and many more – that have told us far more about the Universe than could possibly be imagined.

We have seen planets up close. We have learned about quasars and pulsars, black holes, and supernovas. We have gathered amazing data about how the Universe may have come into being and how it may end. Nothing could be more astonishing.

All our knowledge of the Universe started with ancient people who looked at the sky and wondered. They did not have scientific instruments. They had only their eyes. Even so, they managed to study the objects in the sky and observe how the objects moved. They even reasoned why the movement took place. Our knowledge of the Universe began with these ancient astronomers. We could not have come as far as we have without their early efforts.

Isaac Asimov

A Clear and Pure Sky

In modern times, it is hard to study the night sky. The dust and lights of today's activities hide it. Ancient people had a better, clearer chance to study the sky and see the patterns, or constellations, of the stars.

They drew pictures of constellations that looked like people and animals, and they made up stories to account for the constellations being in the sky. They noticed that the Moon changed its shape from night to night and changed its position against the stars. The earliest calendars, which showed the change of seasons, were based on the changes of the Moon. Ancient priests were among the first astronomers. They studied the sky carefully to make sure the calendars were accurate.

Left: Ancient people were fascinated by the rhythms of the sky. They painted their astronomical observations on the walls of caves.

Early Far Eastern Astronomy

Some stars and constellations, like the Big Dipper, always stay in the same part of the sky. This allowed ancient sailors to use the stars to guide their ships. Polynesians from long ago found their way to distant islands over the vast Pacific Ocean by watching the stars.

In China, too, astronomy was important because changes in the sky were thought to mean future dangerous conditions on Earth. The ancient Chinese astronomers watched for any new stars that might appear, as well as eclipses of the Sun and Moon, so they could warn people of future catastrophic events.

❓ *Lesson of the day*

In the 1400s, a Mongol prince built an observatory and made a star map of 994 stars. It was the best in the world at the time, but its creator was virtually unknown. There must be other unknown ancient astronomers who made great discoveries. For instance, who was the first person to notice Saturn? Who was the first person to determine the coming of the next eclipse? Who was the first person to make an accurate calendar?

Inset, top: Ancient Hawaiians may have used the small island of Kahoolawe near Maui to teach sailors how to navigate by the stars. Archaeologists studying rock carvings on the island found one that looks similar to the constellation Hercules. Another resembles the hooked tail of Scorpius, the Scorpion. Both carvings are over 750 years old.

Inset, bottom: A monument to the magnetic compass, one of China's many early scientific inventions.

Opposite: Using their knowledge of the sea and sky, Polynesian sailors safely crossed the vast Pacific Ocean in fragile boats.

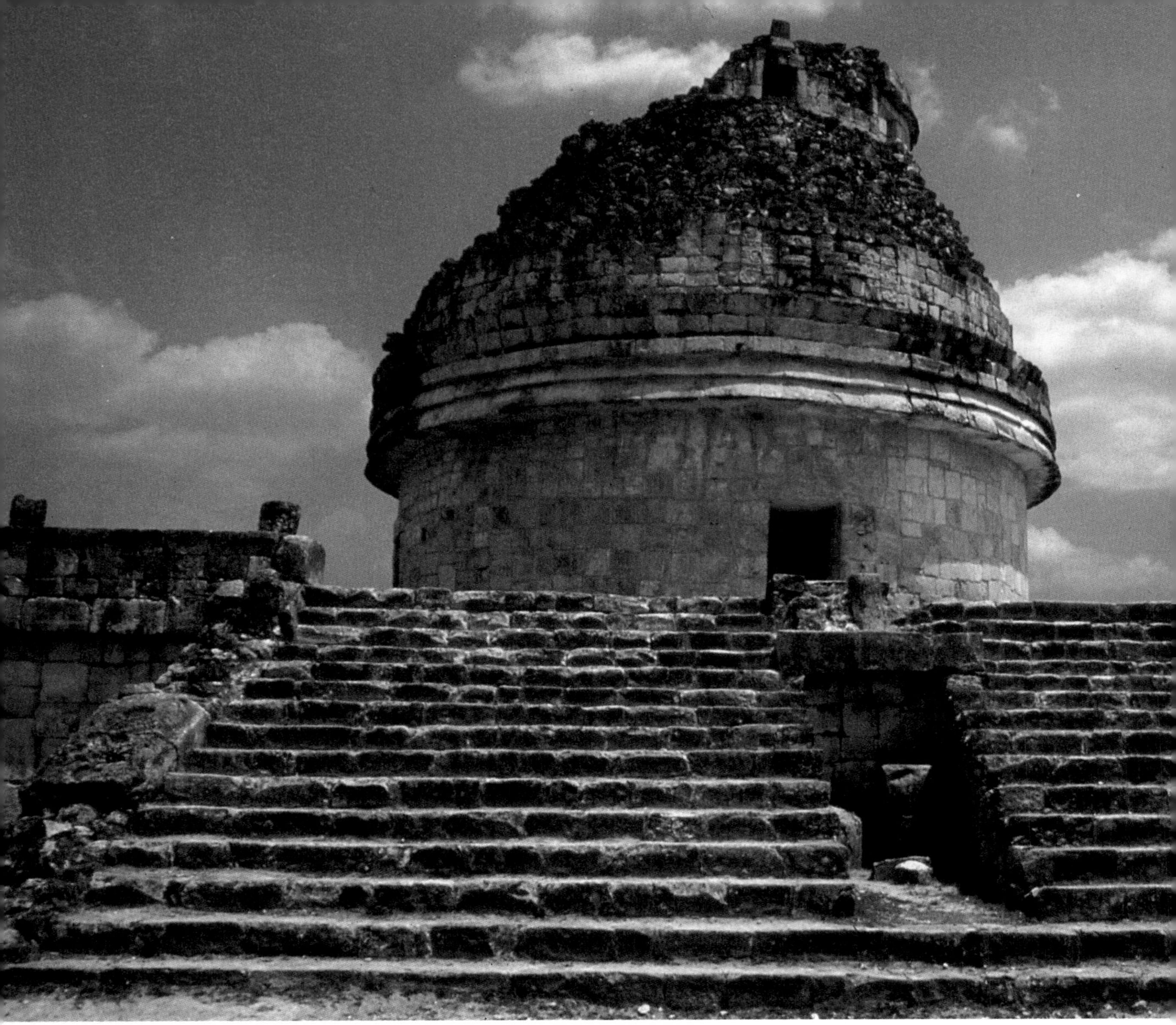

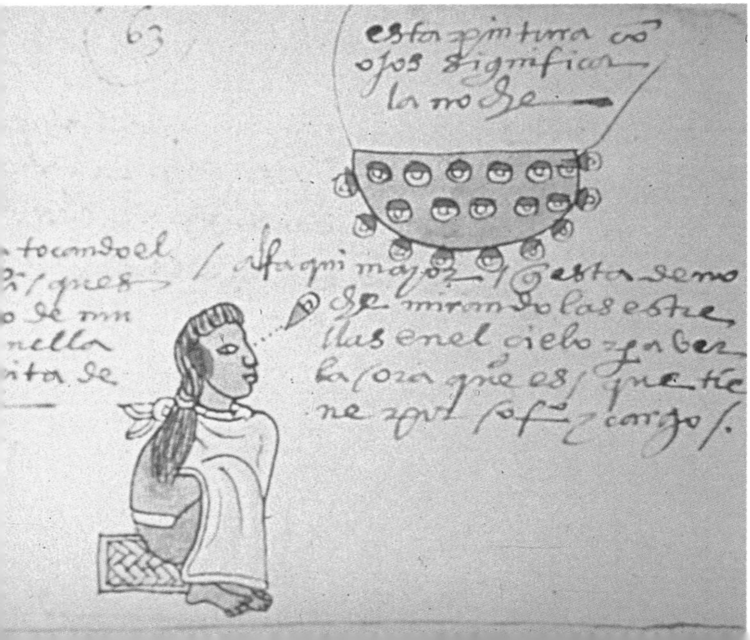
63
esta pintura co ojos significan la noche

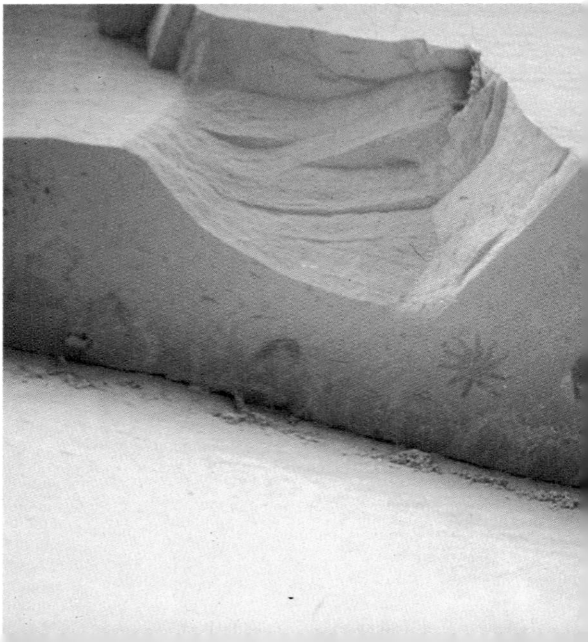

Astronomy in the Early Americas

The early Maya Indians of southern Mexico, Belize, Guatemala, and Honduras developed a complex written language and a clever way of writing numbers. They were the first people in the New World to keep historical records. The Mayans observed the movements of the Sun, the Moon, and the planets – especially Venus. Several of their buildings were designed with the motion of Venus in mind. One of these buildings was even used as an observatory to follow the planet's progress.

The Mayans recorded the cycles they observed from watching the sky in picture books made from tree bark. Only fragments of four of these books survive today, but they clearly show that the Mayans had learned to predict solar and lunar eclipses and the path of Venus. One of the calendars used by the Mayans was even more accurate than the one used by the Spanish when they reached the New World. Most of the books of the great Mayan civilization were destroyed when the Spanish arrived in the early 1500s.

Top: The Caracol of Chichén Itzá, located in northern Yucatán in Mexico, was an early observatory used by the Maya Indians. A thousand years ago, the Mayans studied the movement of the planet Venus through openings in the tower's top.

Far left: The ancient Aztec Indians of Mexico, represented by this Aztec astronomer, used pictographic writing to record their observations of the sky.

Left: Hundreds of years ago, Anasazi Indians drew a sketch of the Moon and a star on the rocks of New Mexico's Chaco Canyon. The drawings may represent the Crab supernova.

Ancient Egypt's Livelihood

The lives of the ancient Egyptians depended on the Nile River. When the river flooded the fields, it was possible for the Egyptians to grow their crops.

Egyptian priests carefully recorded when the floods came – at an interval of every 365 days. So the Egyptians were the first to use a calendar with a 365-day year. The priests also noticed that the bright star Sirius rose with the Sun when the flood was due. The ancient Egyptians also invented sundials to measure the time of day by the movement of the Sun.

? *Now you see'em more; now you see'em less.*

Some stars, called variable stars, seem to get slightly brighter and then dimmer. Why do these stars change in brightness? Some are double stars, and their brightness varies as one member of the pair eclipses, or blocks, the other. Ancient star watchers, *such as the Arabs, might have seen such changes, but they did not speak of them. Why not? These ancients seemed to believe that the heavens never changed, so maybe they did not want to admit that stars could vary in brightness!*

Left: Over four thousand years ago, ancient Egyptians used the position of Sirius to predict the annual flooding of the Nile.

Inset: Sirius is the brightest star in the sky.

Above: Could this have been an ancient observatory? A story in the Bible tells how the people of a Babylonian city tried to build a stairway to the stars – the Tower of Babel.

Predicting the Future in Babylon

Even before the Mayans, the ancient Babylonians were the very first people worldwide to study the movements of the planets Mercury, Venus, Mars, Jupiter, and Saturn. These planets follow complicated paths against the stars.

The Babylonians kept detailed records of these paths and learned to predict them. Like all ancient people, they believed that studying planetary movements gave hints about future happenings on Earth.

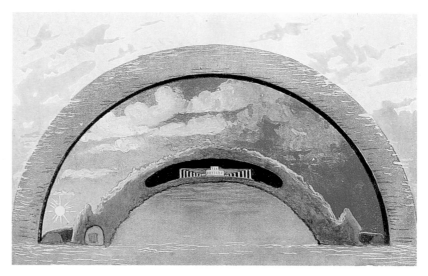

Above: This ancient Babylonian view of the Universe shows a disk of land with water all around. Babylonia is shown at the center of the disk.

The Greeks –
Expanding Babylonian Knowledge

The earliest Greek astronomers probably picked up most of their knowledge from the Babylonians. The Greek philosopher Thales predicted an eclipse of the Sun that took place in 585 B.C. Thales most likely used Babylonian scientific methods to make his prediction.

Around 550 B.C., the Greek philosopher Pythagoras pointed out that the Evening Star and the Morning Star were really the same body. Today, we know that this body is actually the planet Venus. Pythagoras, too, probably used the knowledge of the Babylonians.

But then the Greek astronomers moved ahead. Most people back then thought Earth was flat, but some Greek astronomers thought it might be in the shape of a ball. They also thought the light of the Moon was really reflected sunlight. Today, we know how right they were!

Opposite: The ancient Greek philosopher Pythagoras. His followers were skilled in mathematics and astronomy. They were among the first to think of Earth as a huge ball.

Inset: One early Greek view of the world (hundreds of years before Pythagoras) was a floating disk inside a great hollow ball. The Sun and stars were attached to the ball.

15

Celestial Positions

To the Greeks, Earth was a huge ball at the center of the Universe, and the objects in the sky moved around it in great circles. Each planet moved in a separate circle. The Moon was lowest. Then came Mercury, Venus, the Sun, Mars, Jupiter, and Saturn. The stars were farthest out.

To explain why the planets changed direction, two astronomers, Hipparchus and Ptolemy, developed a detailed scheme of planetary motions. Ptolemy did his work in about A.D. 150. But he used the work of Hipparchus from about 130 B.C. So it took a long time – about 280 years – and a lot of work to come up with ideas about planetary motions. The research was extremely complicated, but it was important information to help determine the movements of the planets.

Opposite, top: Ptolemy thought the Sun, Moon, and planets circled Earth.

Opposite, bottom, right: Ptolemy at work in his Egyptian observatory.

Below: Much of Ptolemy's work is based on that of Hipparchus *(pictured)*, a Greek astronomer who lived over two hundred years before Ptolemy.

⁈ *The world's first star map – just a case of mistaken identity?*

Hipparchus was the first astronomer to make a star map. According to reports, he spotted a new star in 134 B.C. He then made a star map to help identify the stars. But did he really see a new star?

His original reports were destroyed, and there is no record anywhere else of such a star. Not even the Chinese reported it. Should we thank a case of mistaken identity for the first star map?

Early Earthly Statistics

So the ancient Greeks believed Earth was in the shape of a ball. But just how large was Earth and how distant were the other planets from Earth?

In about 240 B.C., a Greek astronomer in Egypt, Eratosthenes, made an exciting discovery. He found that when the Sun was directly overhead in one city, it cast a shadow in another city, about 500 miles (800 kilometers) to the north.

Eratosthenes figured that this meant Earth's surface curved. He also thought Earth was a ball about 25,000 miles (40,000 km) around. Today, we know he was right.

Hipparchus later studied Earth's shadow when it eclipsed the Moon. From the size of the Moon, he decided it must be about 240,000 miles (384,000 km) from Earth. He was right about that, too!

Right: By combining his observations of the sky with his skill in mathematics, Eratosthenes *(opposite)* was able to determine the shape and size of Earth. His first insight regarding this occurred when he compared sunlight in two different cities in Egypt.

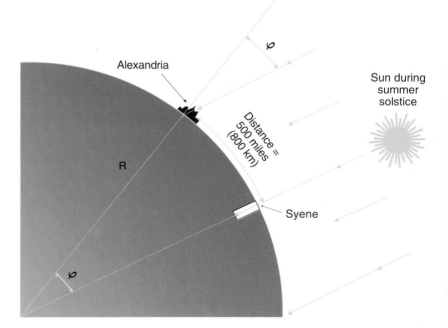

18

Saved by the Arabs

After Ptolemy, Greek science faded and Europe slowly entered a period in time known as the Dark Ages. But the Arabs, beginning in A.D. 632, set up a large empire, discovered Greek books on science and mathematics, translated them into Arabic, and studied them.

Advancements in astronomy were made. In about A.D. 900, an Arab named Al-Battani discovered new ways of determining planetary positions.

In about 1150, Europeans began to translate the Arabic versions of the Greek books into Latin. If it hadn't been for the Arabs, Greek science might have been totally lost!

! *The Dark Ages – they weren't dark everywhere.*

In 1054 for three weeks, a star burned so brightly that it could be seen in daylight. At night, it cast a dim shadow. This supernova, or exploded star, could not be seen very well in the Northern Hemisphere, which partly explains why European and Arab people failed to notice it. But we know of this star because Chinese and Japanese astronomers wrote down their observations of it. Today, it is known as the Crab Nebula.

Opposite: Arabs preserved much of the science of the Greeks.

Top: What is known today as the Crab Nebula was sighted in 1054 in some parts of the world.

Center: Did American Indians record the Crab supernova in 1054? This "supernova bowl" was made by the Mimbres people. It shows a rabbit (a common Moon symbol) near a star surrounded by twenty-three rays. That's the same number of days Chinese astronomers say the supernova could be seen in daylight!

Bottom: Early Greek scientific instruments called astrolabes were refined by the Arabs to help solve difficult problems in astronomy.

21

The Center of the Universe – the Sun

The Greek scheme of the Universe was so complicated that other European astronomers looked for simpler methods. An astronomer from Poland, named Nicolaus Copernicus, decided that a better plan would be to place the Sun at the center of the Universe with the planets circling it.

Earth would have to circle the Sun, too, and this seemed against common sense. But in 1543, Copernicus wrote that his idea would make it much easier to determine planetary positions. For more than fifty years, astronomers argued about whether Copernicus was right or wrong.

Supernova – a star as bright as the Moon

Supernovas are stars that explode in a terrific blaze of light. Sometimes they leave behind a cloud of dust and gas that marks the place of the explosion. One such cloud, called the Gum Nebula, might mark the explosion of a star about 1,500 light-years away. When it was at its peak, about eleven thousand years ago, this star must have shone as brightly as the full Moon. Imagine how astonished people at the time must have been when they saw it!

Opposite: The idea that the Sun, not Earth, was the center of the Universe *(top)* was first stated by Nicolaus Copernicus *(bottom, left).* The Gum Nebula *(bottom, right)* may be what's left of a huge, exploding star.

23

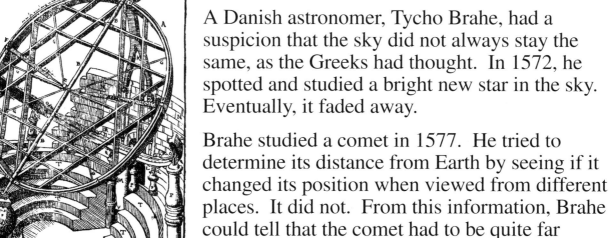

Open to New Viewpoints

A Danish astronomer, Tycho Brahe, had a suspicion that the sky did not always stay the same, as the Greeks had thought. In 1572, he spotted and studied a bright new star in the sky. Eventually, it faded away.

Brahe studied a comet in 1577. He tried to determine its distance from Earth by seeing if it changed its position when viewed from different places. It did not. From this information, Brahe could tell that the comet had to be quite far away, farther than the Moon.

The Greeks had always thought comets were inside our atmosphere. But with updated details about comets from Brahe, early scientists became more open to new ideas about the sky.

! *Comets – ancient astrological enigmas*

Early astronomers did not know very much about comets. Comets appeared suddenly, moved against the stars unpredictably, and then vanished. People thought they might be special warnings of disaster. It wasn't until 1705

that an English astronomer, Edmund Halley, explained the motions of comets, showing they moved around the Sun in unusual, but predictable, orbits. Even so, some people are still frightened by comets.

Opposite: Tycho Brahe witnessed the explosion of a star in 1572. He recorded the position of this supernova so precisely that modern astronomers have found its remains *(inset)*.

Top: Tycho Brahe built this huge instrument, an armillae, to measure the positions of the stars and planets.

Bottom: English astronomer Edmund Halley explained the motions of the comets.

An Astronomical Turning Point

A turning point in astronomy came with the invention of the telescope in Holland in 1608. An Italian astronomer, Galileo Galilei, heard about the new invention and built his own. In 1609, he pointed it toward the heavens.

Immediately, Galileo discovered many stars that were too dim to see without a telescope. He also found that the Moon was an entire world – with craters, mountains, and what looked like seas. He found that the planet Jupiter had four moons that moved around it, and that Venus changed shape, just as the Moon did.

This new information didn't fit the Greek views of astronomy, but it did fit the views of Copernicus. At that moment, modern astronomy began!

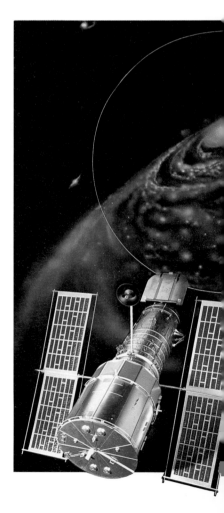

Opposite: Galileo experiments with his first telescope.

Inset: The Hubble Space Telescope vastly improves our ability to observe the Universe.

Fact File:
Astronomy – Past and Present

The earliest observatories may have been simply open platforms where astronomers could watch the sky with no buildings in the way.

At least five thousand years ago, ancient astronomers began using large stones arranged in rows or circles to chart how the Sun and stars moved through the sky. The most famous ancient observatory of this kind is a circle of large upright stones called Stonehenge, in England. American Indians also built circles of stones they lined up with the Sun and stars to determine when the Sun would rise and when summer would start.

An observatory built in Egypt in about 300 B.C. might have contained early instruments like the astrolabe. Greek and Arab astronomers used the astrolabe – which means "star-finder" – to sight and predict the movements of the Sun, Moon, planets, and stars, and to tell time.

Before the telescope was invented, perhaps the most advanced observatory of all was the one founded by the Danish astronomer Tycho Brahe in the late 1500s. It used long, open sighting devices to watch the sky.

The telescope was the beginning of modern astronomy. Today, in addition to optical telescopes, astronomers use instruments that pick up radio waves from objects too far away for us to see very well. These instruments have even been launched into space for closer observations of celestial objects. The instruments make discoveries that ancient astronomers never dreamed of.

A brief history of observatories from prehistoric days to the present:

▲ 3000 B.C. – Stonehenge, England

▲ 30,000 years ago – Cave drawings by early humans

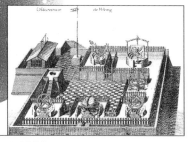

▲1100 –
Chichén Itzá,
Yucatán, Mexico

▲1576 –
Tycho Brahe's observatory,
Ven, Denmark

.D. 1000 –
y American
e alignments

▲1600s –
Beijing Observatory,
China

◀1724 –
Delhi Observatory, India

▼1967 – Mauna Kea
Observatory, Hawaii

▲1838 –
Pulkova
Observatory,
St. Petersburg,
Russia

'80s –
ervatory in Quito,
ador

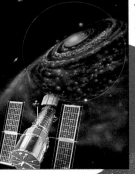

◀1990s –
Hubble Space
Telescope

More Books about Astronomy

Astronomy Basics. Paton (Franklin Watts)
The Macmillan Book of Astronomy. Gallant (Macmillan)
Modern Astronomy. Asimov (Gareth Stevens)
Sky Watchers of Ages Past. Weiss (Houghton Mifflin)
Space Explorers. Asimov (Gareth Stevens)
A Stargazer's Guide. Asimov (Gareth Stevens)

Videos

Ancient Astronomy. (Gareth Stevens)
Astronomy Today. (Gareth Stevens)

Places to Visit

You can explore the same parts of the cosmos that fascinated ancient astronomers – without leaving Earth. Here are some museums and centers where you can find a variety of space exhibits.

NASA Lewis Research Center
Educational Services Office
21000 Brookpark Road
Cleveland, OH 44135

Henry Crown Space Center
Museum of Science and Industry
57th Street and Lake Shore Drive
Chicago, IL 60637

Perth Observatory
Walnut Road
Bickley, W.A. 6076 Australia

Ontario Science Centre
770 Don Mills Road
Don Mills, Ontario M3C 1T3

NASA Lyndon B. Johnson Space Center
2101 NASA Road One
Houston, TX 77058

National Air and Space Museum-Smithsonian
Seventh Street and Independence Avenue SW
Washington, D.C. 20560

Places to Write

Here are some places you can write for more information about astronomy. Be sure to state what kind of information you would like. Include your full name and address so they can write back to you.

Sydney Observatory
P. O. Box K346
Haymarket 2000 Australia

The Planetary Society
65 North Catalina
Pasadena, CA 91106

National Museum of Science and Technology
P. O. Box 9724
Station T
Ottawa, Ontario K1G 5A3

National Space Society
922 Pennsylvania Avenue SE
Washington, D.C. 20003

Glossary

annual: happening once a year.

armillae: a scientific instrument used to measure the positions of the stars and planets.

astrolabe: "star-finder" – an instrument once used to solve problems of astronomy, including the distances of the Sun and other celestial objects from Earth.

astronomy: the scientific study of the various bodies of the Universe.

atmosphere: the gases that surround some planets. Earth's atmosphere consists of oxygen, nitrogen, carbon dioxide, and other gases.

calendar: a system for dividing time, most commonly into days, weeks, and months. Every calendar has a starting day and ending day for a year.

comet: an object made of ice, rock, and gas with a tail that may be seen when the object comes near the Sun. Early people often believed comets predicted Earthly disasters.

constellations: groupings of stars in the sky that seem to trace familiar patterns or figures. Constellations are named after the shapes they resemble.

Dark Ages: a popular name for the early part of the Middle Ages. The Dark Ages covered a period of several hundred years that is often associated with a lack of learning throughout Europe.

eclipse: the total or partial blocking of light that occurs when one heavenly body crosses the shadow of another. During a solar eclipse, parts of Earth are in the shadow of the Moon as the Moon cuts across the Sun and hides it from Earth for a period of time.

nebula: a vast cloud of dust and gas in the Universe.

observatory: a building or site designed and equipped with scientific instruments for the study of astronomy.

planet: one of the celestial bodies that revolves around our Sun.

star map: a chart showing prominent stars and constellations.

sundial: an instrument to measure the time of day by the movement and location of the Sun.

supernova: the violent death of a large star in which most of its gas is blown into space in an explosion as bright as a galaxy.

telescope: an instrument usually made of lenses or mirrors used to observe distant objects.

Tower of Babel: according to the Bible, a huge tower built by people who thought they could reach the heavens by climbing higher and higher into the sky.

Index

Born in 1920, Isaac Asimov came to the United States as a young boy from his native Russia. As a young man, he was a student of biochemistry. In time, he became one of the most productive writers the world has ever known. His books cover a spectrum of topics, including science, history, language theory, fantasy, and science fiction. His brilliant imagination gained him the respect and admiration of adults and children alike. Sadly, Isaac Asimov died shortly after the publication of the first edition of *Isaac Asimov's Library of the Universe*.

The publishers wish to thank the following for permission to reproduce copyright material: front cover, © M. Timothy O'Keefe/Tom Stack and Associates; 4-5, © Garret Moore 1987; 6-7 (upper), © Rowland B. Reeve; 6-7 (lower), Wu-Pen/Mme Ye-Shu-Hua; 7, Bishop Museum; 8, Science Photo Library; 8-9 (upper), © Frank Reddy; 8-9 (lower), United States Geological Survey; 10-11, © Kurt Burmann 1988; 11, © Frank Zullo; 12-13, Kunsthistorisches Museum; 13, Mary Evans Picture Library; 14-15, Ann Ronan Picture Library; 15, The Granger Collection, New York; 16-17, Ann Ronan Picture Library; 17 (both), Mary Evans Picture Library; 18, Gérard Franquin/© Père Castor; 19, © Mark Maxwell 1988; 20, The Granger Collection, New York; 21 (upper), The Crab Nebula, Messier 1, From plates of the Hale 5m telescope, © Malin/Pasachoff/Caltech 1992; 21 (center), Collection Frederick R. Weisman Art Museum at the University of Minnesota, Minneapolis; 21 (lower), Adler Planetarium; 23 (upper), Mary Evans Picture Library; 23 (lower left), The Granger Collection, New York; 23 (lower right), Science Photo Library; 24 (large), Ann Ronan Picture Library; 24 (inset), National Optical Astronomy Observatories; 25 (upper), Paris Observatory; 25 (lower), Courtesy of Julian Baum; 26-27, Space Telescope Science Institute; 27, The Granger Collection, New York; 28 (upper), Science Photo Library; 28 (lower), 29 (upper left), © Garret Moore 1987; 29 (top center), Mary Evans Picture Library; 29 (upper right), © Frank Reddy; 29 (center left), Courtesy of Julian Baum; 29 (second from top, right), Mary Evans Picture Library; 29 (lower left), Science Photo Library; 29 (bottom center), © Greg Vaughn/Tom Stack and Associates; 29 (second from bottom, right), Courtesy of Julian Baum; 29 (lower right), Space Telescope Science Institute.